# Said the Cannibal:
## Poems with Bite

Laurie Smith

For Kevin: a man after my own heart! Love Laurie

Crossroads Poetry Series
Three Fires Confederacy Territory
Windsor, Ontario, Canada

First Edition. October 2017

Library and Archives Canada Cataloguing in Publication

Smith, Laurie, 1956-, author
Said the cannibal : tongue in cheek / Laurie Smith.

Poems.
ISBN 978-1-988214-18-4 (softcover)

I. Title.

PS8587.M55274S25 2017 C811'.54 C2017-906684-6

Book Layout: D.A. Lockhart

Published in the United States of America and Canada by

Urban Farmhouse Press
www.urbanfarmhousepress.com

The Crossroads Poetry Series is a line of books that showcases established and emerging poetic voices from across North America. The books in this series represent what the editors at UFP believe to be some of the strongest voices in both American and Canadian poetics. *Said the Cannibal* is the eighth book in this series.

Printed in Adobe Garamond Pro font

*For Dan and Emily*

# Contents

*"There are people who eat the earth and eat all the people on it like in the Bible with the locusts. And other people who stand around and watch them eat."*

-Lillian Hellman

## a ponder

if you ever get stuck in a bear trap,
or for instance
with your arm or leg wedged
between a rock and a hard place,
and your best recourse is to chew off
your own arm or leg to escape,
does that count as cannibalism, or
just if you swallow?

and further to that,
would the one being consumed
actually have to die and be digested
in order for this to meet the legal requirements
or can little bits and strips be vivisected
as needed, piecemeal, if you will?

also, those vulgar terms applied to human
sexual pleasures, the tasting, eating,
comparison to meat or juicy ripe peaches etc.,
i wonder where one draws the line.

the reason i ask is i do bite
my nails.

## eye candy

i used to collect
candy eyes,
the colourful little
embellishments on
easter bunnies,
lambs, duckies,
chicks.

most people
go for the ears first.
but i preferred to blind them
so they couldn't foresee
the rest.

the eyes were never meant to be
eaten.
i just liked to periodically
take out the tiny white
cardboard box and
admire my accumulation
of yellow, blue, pink, green, black
irises on ovals and discs of
hard royal icing.

so pretty to look at.

## eating pink grapefruit

why did grade six boys make
grapefruit seem like something
dirty?

it sits on the countertop, nipple up
and i imagine there should be two.
bigger than lemons, oranges. grapefruits!

i only want to cut into it.
breakfast.
that is all.

a serrated knife creates a pair of
blushing flowers,
seeds like teardrops halved,
its fragrance becomes the kitchen;
i would close my eyes but for that knife.

there are many ways to proceed:
the careful removal of membrane, pith,
scooping out clear segments with a spoon
– all so tedious.

i prefer to divide each half into
five perfect wedges,
sprinkle generously with white sugar.
no idea when i learned this

i only know i don't want to
wring the juice out with my hands.

## funny ha-ha

remember how funny cannibalism used to be
on gilligan's island? and in the cartoons –
three dark-skinned [restless] natives
(either skinny or well-nourished, depending on the plot)
with bones in their kinky hair, rings through their noses,
wearing grass skirts
maybe loin cloths (depending on the location)

but it was usually africa
or some remote south seas island

anyway, there they were dancing
around a big black cauldron
stoking the fire,
while some hapless rope-bound white guy
screamed for help

we laughed so hard.

## babycakes

do babies really like it
when grandma or great aunty
sticks her wrinkly face
nose distance from him
so close she spits, her teeth a jigglin'
fly tracks and fingerprints evident
on her specs and

in that scratchy cartoon granny voice
with jowls afluffin' and head abobbin'
sing-songs *you're just so scrumptious,*
*i could almost eat you!*
*i'm gonna gobble you up!*
the inflection rising with each
effusive threat?

## grim

once upon a time in a deep dark wood
there were two very naughty children
who wandered off before their chores were done and
getting hungry came across a cottage made of candy,
took a bite of windowsill, tried doormat, mailbox,
oh, come in said the hostess to her visitors
i've cookies baking in the oven,
look closer, she cackles,
guess what you're it!

upon one time in autumn, likely
based in part by bright red hooded cloak
and contents of the goody basket, there went
skipping off to grandma's -- Little was her name,
a pleasant girl, well meaning, but alas she
could have been devoured by a wicked wolf
so the village grownups warned unruly brats
respect your elders or
who knows?

and once upon another time three billy goats
were bound to cross a bridge the troll
below said wait, the toll to pass is goat
pick one amongst yourselves but really
those who told this story once again meant
naughty little children.

# ALTERNATIVE HISTORY

I'm very glad you're here!
[said the native to the castaway.]

You do look like you're in a bit of a stew, my good man.

Indeed, sir, your timing is impeccable;
my colleagues were about to light a match
and set the home fires at slow and dreadful simmer.
They'll be back anon with fuel and condiments.

Alas, we can't have that; what say your name young fellow
(and BTW, where ever will they find a book of matches in this
godforsaken jungle?)

(Here, loosen this.) I have no name but you can call me Monday
to celebrate the moment of my rescue. And to whom
will I owe my very life?

Robinson Crusoe as my father's implement, yet
I must note, according to my journal notes we now
mark Wednesday.

Oh dear, I must have blacked out in that commotion on the beach,
intruders with their strange canoes and fire sticks.
Might you tell me what I missed?

Well, your unkind kind have vanquished them, yet now it seems
you're taken for a coward having fainted in the heat of battle
which I observed from there beyond the trees, and come to
free you. Hurry now.

Thank God it's Wednesday, Crusoe, and we've made it o'er that hump!
I pledge myself to serve in any way you deem.

Great, I'll lend you pants, put you to work at heavy lifting
and I wonder, can you cook?

Of course, my dish of choice is slow and seasoned long pig,
roasted over coals a good two days.

Aha, that sounds delightful!
So then, dinner Friday?

## palm sunday

there she's off to services,
again this year will bring home a consecrated frond
to dehydrate and crumble on her mantle,
*i brought you one, for luck*
*it's from jerusalem, and even*
*our bishop has blessed it*

*oh, how thoughtful*

i recall those giddy catholic girls down the block,
holier than moi when they took their vows
of first communion, described to me their wedding
dresses and veils, their new saintly names given
as they prepared to be married to jesus
and i wanted to know how could they have his babies
if he already died on a cross
besides they are only nine years old, what if…

you're so ignorant.

and what about that fantastic privilege now
of confessing all your sins, off the hook
for breaking rules like
you can only have candy on sundays
when you get home from church

*but how hungry would you be*
*after free wine and crackers?*

*it's the blood and body of christ!*
they rolled their eyes in explanation

i said they were cannibals then if they ate a human body
or vampires if they drank blood,
but no it's symbolism they proclaimed, using other big words
like eucharist and transubstantiation,

hell i just believed they were far too young
to be drinking the wine.

## roller skating to timothy, 1971

**Rupert Holmes/The Buoys*

we buzzed merrily on a smooth grey rink
all summer the *mine-had-caved-in*
thought nothing of those lyrics because the beat was perfect

and the roar of two thousand wheels negated the fact
joe and the other buoys would *sell their souls for a piece*
*of meat* since many of us were hungry
after standing in tight circles outside passing joints back and forth
or swigging watered down whisky from silver flasks

it was even better if one of the two tims i knew showed up
and somebody requested the song; we would all sing it real loud,
*timothy, timothy, god what did we do*? laugh and point
out that little tim was all skin and bone, we'd starve for sure,
big tim would blush with embarrassment at the attention,
and guys named joe just shrugged.

but afterwards we'd pile in somebody's brother's car and head to
macdonalds for big macs and fries with too much ketchup
totally forgetting that *nobody ever got around*
to asking tim if he wanted to come.

## performance art

tonsil canapés
finger sandwiches
sliced testicles
in hot sauce
cheesy kneecaps

crunchy cartilage
minced kidney pies
spiced organ meat
light dinner music

toe dancing after
cock tails and fat
candlelight by camera
and an audience

of epicurious
gluttons

**In Vancouver, artist Rick Gibson, after a few attempts intercepted by police was finally able to eat a donated testicle (presumably not his own) in 1989.*

## found poetry

### Family of Man Found Biting Murder Victim's Face Off Offer Condolences: 'There Are No Words'

that's how you find it.
just open your web browser.
you don't have to look far
and it really does jump up to
bite you in the face.

accompanying photo was not nearly
as graphic as anticipated.

some fbi excuses were offered
about superhuman strength and synthetic drugs
pending toxicology reports.

but a guy killed a couple. then tried to
gnaw off the husband's face!

this actually happens.

## bodyworks

from the main body
we have
a riverbank
an arm
a committee
a paragraph
a pancreas
a brisket
a mind

## extinction

what's the problem?
it's always happened
no room here for all
past and present species ->
future evolutions to exist
at the same time.

dodo, dinosaurs gone, so?
why do we humans care about
polar bears, pandas (cute furry things)
insects, microbes…

because we know,
we feel SELFconscious,
conscience, guilt
or

it could happen to us.

indeed, it will.  we're only a blip
but in the meanwhile
we do hate for things to change.

## as in sweeney todd

i've lately
(why, you ask?)
been in the cold backrooms of butcher shops
where half animals hang
all rosy, magenta and off-white sinew,
ribby-striped just out of reach,

conveyed on hooks
they look like they could knock you out
on impact
sprawl you on the sticky floor
atop the dogfood byproducts.

hard to guess the weight of meat
until it's sawed and hacked
to shoulder chops or porterhouse or
little chunks of stewing beef.

these body parts are given new names
as they're transformed from guilt to palatable.
how easy might it be to eat another human
if the flesh was faceless, served in bite-sized morsels.

## "Grand Champion Steer"

*will dress out nicely*
says the auctioneer.
i'm not sure what that means, but
do the math--
starting bid $1.25 a pound @ 1,325 lbs,
consider the additional costs:
styrofoam trays, absorption pads, plastic wrap…

his ears pierced, labeled, flaring
nostrils wet, wide with the country
fair aroma of BBQ, hot dogs, burgers
in the next aisle, sad-eyed
sold at a buck 92

led away ignorantly,
i wonder

the black angus passing him on the way in
is a belligerent 1278 lbs.
shit caked under his tail
rebels at the rope
mocks the audience *i dare you* he bellows,
*eat this, jerk,*
*you don't know where I've been,*
*what i drank last night*
$1.70/ lb.

next up is "Thunder"
so docile while little Abby Anger takes the mic
to thank her grandpa and grandma and the sponsors
for all the support she got from 4H over the years.
her pink-haltered pet slobbers like a rabid black bear,
staggering in the heat

craps, poses
under the shade tree in the corner of the sale ring
for the professional photographer shooting him
next to his proud buyers.

## frenzy

chickens
cooped
wired
little octagons
sturdy as the 2x2
corner posts

foxes climb,
burrow
clucking victims
scramble like grain, corn
scramble like eggs
that lived long enough

barnyard politics
about walls
stalls
balls hacked off,
heads on chopping blocks
cows coming home
to roost
barn doors closed

## dream: 7:21am: futureworld

location:  dude ranch.
play cowboys
put you in line for your initiation…
clinical, and there are nurses.
a grey upholstered chair.
they brace your legs and arms
in padded clamps.

    (yes, dear, this will hurt
    quite a bit, but you'll be
    sedated
    and kept overnight, feel better
    in the morning)

it's branding –
you're branding them!

a scream
from the last young fellow
he sobs in the next room

but why?

    (you must, for your children.  how will they know you?)

my children do know me
    i want a tattoo.

    (no, dear, this is better, lasts forever on the
        red muscled flesh of your thigh.)

i want a tattoo; i know what i want.
    i choose!

    (but dear, your children…if you ever…get separated,
    like the sheep, how do the little calves find
    mothers all named Bessie and Rachel and Belle?)

then the cowboys and the shepherds should read more books,
be more imaginative in the naming of their livestock.

*a whisper:* (what does it matter
when your mother
is probably meat?)

## dream: Mimi the Potbelly Pig

I was rounding the corner of Seminole at Pillette, east to north, I think, and ran out of gas. Got out, beside Mimi, to push her into the gas station at Beckers and as I was coaxing her up the grade, up to the pumps, she turned into a bristly, squirming
potbelly pig, black and prickly and quite uncooperative. I half-rode her into what is not in reality a service bay, and said to the attendant, One pound, please.
He took her into a back room, put her on a table and proceeded to draw on the squealing hellion two sliver shapes, parallel to her spine, but so as not to include backbone or ribs. This is where I will cut, he said, are you sure one pound will be enough? What about anaesthetic, I asked, concerned for my beloved pet. Oh, we never mind, they make a racket, but they pass out…it's best not to spoil them, they do get
used to it after the first time, anyway. I think I will become a vegetarian, I said. Please get her off the table.

Interpretation – later that day

Car repairs can be a pain.

## new york, 2022

soylent green
takes place five years from now.
inconceivable.

conceivable.
look at this mess.

dystopian literature
is hot and
children play at zombie apocalypse
i guess the same as we used to pretend war,
pointing our fingers,
ratatatatatat…you're dead.

like on tv.
of course this is just make believe.

i'm afraid. past useful so
yes, i'll admit it, i'm afraid.

it's all about the packaging
of those green protein wafers.

## don’t breathe a word

there are skeletons in my closet
a feast for the eyes,
if you have the heart
not so much skin as bones
you see, i have a sweet tooth
and blood is thicker than wine,
i wash my hands of this.

## muffin top

you have a muffin top
and there's been a zombie apocalypse or nuclear holocaust
and the earth is frozen around your cave where
only your family is left to repopulate the world
and all the dogs and cats and squirrels
and rats have been eaten now your grandchildren are
gnawing on tree bark and shoe leather in desperation so

do you sacrifice yourself entirely

or just let someone cut away the flabby parts while
you're biting on a rock?
underarm wings like chicken,
pork belly rolls an easy  two slits and makeshift duct tape
pulling the seams back together you won't miss it,
(always wanted to lose the spare tire)
lumpy steaks from inner thighs,
a block of ice between your legs to numb the pain

and the kids would never have to know, you'll sit
huddled in a corner and tell them stories to pass the time,
while the hearty now are able to venture farther afield
for something flammable
or to look for other survivors, plump and friendly.

## child support

this is for the absent fathers
the sperm donors
layabouts
absconders of freedom

lucky  your mate is not the black widow spider
because if she spat on you
as deserved
you'd be finished

paralyzed and hollowed out slowly
by the hundreds of hatchlings
swarming your nutritious lap  like a jungle gym
climbing and gnawing at your hairy legs
as you watch  through not dead compound eyes
until even those are consumed

there is no longer the joy of  seeing
your offspring frolic
on your numb misery

think of your daughters
sometimes  think of your daughters
and hope they find such
altruistic sires for your descendants

## fava

there is sometimes a vicious base
hostile urge
a voracious rage that curls lips back
bares canines and tongue dripping
with the  anticipatory lubricant,

i will tear you to pieces
starting at the throat
a good shake of sense too late
you'll serve best as fodder,
protein sustenance

but with your plump body limp
at my feet, eyes glazed over
arms and legs an abstract posture
i think now your mustard sweater
is a turnoff
tight thighs an unappealing meal
care not to rip into your flesh
with my mouth

in disgust i would ask for this
carcass to be carried off,
drained and dressed properly
presented with formal dinnerware
and the correct wine

## the cull

i prepare for my own barbarity,
close my eyes and run water, wash my hands
pilate-like,
deny, excuse
there is precedent and adamic permission
god has said that man may rule, may take
what meat is necessary for his own good,
in his own name
for the sake of the
herd

stalking the primitive
i am
cold becomes me
for as long as it must take then
gun raised to shoulder, peace,
i say, on
snowy earth the immediate titian spill,
the rugged drop and clatter of antlers,

shocking silence

## the Donner Party

Dasher Dancer Prancer Vixen
Comet Cupid Rudolph Blitzen.
So, Donner. hosted the reindeer games,
the big post season blowout in the snowy woods.
berries and twigs aplenty,
take-out cookies and carrots a luxury,
tree sap running,

'til things got out of hand, seems
Prancer left her bell at Rudolph's place
but it was really a setup, a conspiracy between
Dasher and Vixen, get Blitzen's goat
by making him think Prancer was steppin' out,
arrogant bastard jealous of Rudy's promotion,
he should've just let it go.
Who would think he'd wrap her in his harness,
disbelieve her fauning eyes,
her dying breath a frosty rising cloud

the others storm in too late as
typical of these tragic winter tales.
well that's enough the buck stops here
they clash like swordsmen in the forest
antlers slashing cloven hooves
thrashing blindly roaring vengeance for
dear innocence

and when the fog is lifting there is
little venison left upon the bones
now strewn across the bloody snow.

## carnage

it looks like the aftermath of a terrorist attack
in my bedroom
torsos, legs, feet, faux mink furs,
black plastic pedestals, decapitations

some will only be identifiable by matching
what's left of their clothes to the pictures
on the collector boxes I've been saving
to augment their value.

or dental records, no,
those are coonhound puppy teeth marks,
the morning after the night i told myself
I really should put my complete set of Barbie figurines
out of reach

## only rats

this plan can't work
it's as old as plague,
the hopping of rat fleas
scratch dance insipid
vile

meticulous this
strategy for destruction,

it can't work,
they will guess and find
a cure,
find a prevention
preemption

the dock cats
will see the rat coming
slink and pounce
put an end to
festering
eyes

only cats can
save us

## cure for epilepsy, 15th century

european renaissance
blood sucking vampires
hung around
the foot of false dawn    gallows
pewter mugs and   golden chalices in hand
to catch the slosh and splatter
as common heads were    rolling,

toast the dead with   gratitude
black market drug   in hand
the cure for
falling
sickness
a transfusion thick upon their lips

fly off in velvet or in dingy cloaks
by sunrise and
defer the madness
some will chase it down with wine

## mumia

some english verbs are stupid
like “they practiced cannibalism.”

it takes practice?
like, “the practice of medicine.”
oh, i see the connection:

mummified false kings pulverized
and dispensed by kilogram,

the alchemy of skull moss,
scraped from air dried crania and
used as poultice.

blood potions
promoted by 17th century euro-elite,
the same who might burn those
who practiced witchcraft.

semantics.

## kuru

women and children first
have the honour of
consuming the brains of the
deceased to ingest their spirits

guard with their fore
shortened lives

but deadly prions
infiltrate their nervous systems
lay dormant for years
'til finally like mad cows they
begin to twitch and stagger
laugh at nothing
and starve themselves

within the year they too
will die and be mourned
while the oblivious population
spirals thus
to near extinction

## how they dealt with politicians in 1672

background is unnecessary, it's so common.
a country in unrest,
the middle class blaming the elite
somebody charges the other guy with treason
but he's still got pull and after the
prescribed period of thumbscrew interviews,
foot burning or water boarding
his well positioned brother
finagles his release into exile

this doesn't sit well with administration,
so as the de witt boys were being transferred
the cops probably fired the first shot
busied themselves elsewhere
and let the mob have at them

they stripped and mutilated the bodies
hung them feet first on a convenient gibbet
roasted their livers, and shared the meat
in what was called a disciplined frenzy,
a choreography of cannibals.

yes, it was a time of culture and prosperity,
religious tolerance and civilized dissent,
demands, purgings, the raising of eyebrows and
the turning of heads.

## the siege of fort detroit, may 1763

this is close to home,
and the weather around here in may
is quite lovely

perhaps conspicuous to try smuggling weapons
into the fort under heavy woven blankets;
the british are ready, pontiac withdraws.

comes back two days later,
grabs some gladwin soldiers
on the way in, stops for lunch.
ritual intimidation. but never eat the french.

brits hold their ground. await
cuyler's convoy, unaware their supplies
had been intercepted at point pelee

until the bloody flotilla of captives arrives
on the river. bloated corpses have a way
of affecting the morale of even the most
seasoned army.

## polyphasia

*Tarrare (c. 1772 – 1798)*

so you want something morbid, serious?
bloody and despicable?
let's get real.

i'll take you back to late 18th century France.
a lot of boys were hungry, but this kid
could eat his own weight in beef
in a single day
was thrown out of the house

and wandered to Paris in the company of
hookers and charlatans who
capitalized on his talent for
shoving a dozen eggs in his lipless mouth at once
eating wine corks and stones
baskets of apples, snake meat,
live rats…

impressive show put on by a scrawny
youth and audiences would revel at how
his skin would hang loose as his tunic
until fed, when like a balloon the body would
distend, eyes would go bloodshot
and a putrid vapour would emanate from
his sweating bulk.

sated, he'd lay lethargic as the machine of
his digestion would belch and fart,
spew diarrhea  and continue to grind
jaws ready for the next refueling.
other than that, observers say he appeared
normal.

he was studied and tested
by way of meat pies enough for fifteen men
washed down with gallon jugs of milk,
thirty pounds of raw bulls' lungs and livers
served in a wheelbarrow

lizards, puppies,
a cat was proffered live
he tore it open with his blood stained teeth
sucked its bones from inside out and
vomited up the fur.
the French army saw a use for this
and fed him messages to mule
in little wooden boxes, defecated contents
found legible behind the Prussian lines
led to a noose placed round his neck.

reprieved and beaten he returned
to hospital, sought treatment
in laudanum and vinegar,
tobacco pills, soft-boiled eggs.

but this flesh eating disease was
not within the realm of current science, and helpless
he would leave his room at night to fight stray dogs
in back of butcher shops, or over gutter carrion.

was caught eating used poultices in the clinic.
was caught drinking blood from patients in phlebotomy,
was caught dining in the morgue.
one night a toddler disappeared, and
Tarrare was finally sent away.

four years later he came back to beg
relief, told doctors he believed a golden fork was
lodged inside him causing all his suffering,
but they recognized consumption in its
final stages.

his rotting corpse repulsive yet an irony
explored, abnormal stomach full
of ulcers, but the golden fork was never found.

## famine

in leached ground, bones dry
faster, all meat hastened clean
by ravenous worms.

## the baby eaters

Swift's modest proposal,
to eat plump Irish toddlers
a satiric English lesson
in pragmatics

yet there are times,
were times, to be generous…
we have surely evolved
past the desperate infanticide
of Saturn's paranoia?

there are stories of trading infants
in China and Russia,
stories they don't want to tell,
(but no one had to eat their own
during times of paucity.)

there are recent documents and statistics
of learned rituals, survival cannibalism
filial sacrifice:
fingers, thighs, breasts
give until it hurts, save our souls.

there are historical records,
culturally endorsed prescriptions
and recipes.

## Jane who was eaten

*"And now famin beginneinge to Looke gastely and pale in every face, thatt notheinge was Spared to mainteyne Lyfe and to doe those things which seame incredible, as to digge upp deade corpes outt of graves and to eate them."* – George Percy

in the starving time, they waited perhaps until the weakest finally let go,
(this is long after the horses and the dogs,
cats, rats, mice…

shoe leather.)

Jane is fourteen, alone,
possibly the daughter of a gentleman, or indentured help
obliged to join the family on this great adventure,
see Virginia,

start over

it was a rough crossing, only six ships made it past the Azores, then
those who hadn't been thrown overboard
expected gracious respite when they finally came ashore at Jamestown,

bad timing. the travel brochures don't mention drought
or the hostile Powhatan, or the fact that the 38 men who'd toughed out
the past two winters here were counting on you to bring your own supplies, maybe
loaves and fishes.

Jane, don't step outside the fortress gates to seek the promised milk and honey,
don't drink the toxic water
and despite your hunger don't sip the blood of any man as he lies dying,

don't turn your back to the door at night if
you need to close your eyes.

the cut marks on her skull suggest the butchers were unskilled
yet had the decency to turn her face away before they
harvested her protein rich brain, the meat of sallow cheeks.

Jane, could you know there'd be survivors,
and you would be the hero of pioneers?

## raft of the medusa

the word 'clinging'
is often used in reference
to life
boats,
rafts

days and nights spent
searing,
searching any horizon,
(it is all horizon)

becomes the madness of tigers
and meerkats
wafts of smoke in the distance,
whiff of rotting legs

the pragmatics of literature
drift on our
fascination with despair

from the moment that great wave
washes over
or the rope is severed
there are conflicting views of
protocol, privilege

access to the high ground,
blood and body.
often the foresight to include casks of wine
so days are endless

some slip away in the night
others wake to find themselves
aboard bright vessels, saved
for the telling of tales.

## winter in Canada: Franklin expedition, 1847

i am making soup.
from the living room i hear weather updates:
subzero windchills all day, stay inside.
comfort food

there was a kettle of beef broth in my fridge;
i'd boiled bones for the dogs on sunday
and planned for this.
barley, potatoes, canned tomatoes, onions
a pinch of chili pepper for heat.

those poor men.
lead-crazed desperate,
yet we pass judgment based on forensics,
cut marks consistent with de-fleshing
and pot polished bone ends, femurs, tibia,
too long for the cauldron, rubbing against the sides
evidence of a last ditch attempt to extract
what marrow might sustain them.

i envision the survivors
holding their hands over the steam
while they watch.

## winter at truckee lake

donner party
of 87
sounds like dinner reservations
at an overcrowded denny's

road trip bypass, who's hungry?
some guy said he knows a shortcut
off the I-80, get us there in half the time…

hi-way still under construction;
split up, we'll meet in the parking lot
pitch a tent, hunker down for the long
wait

## Belsen

I was marched past
this wall of almost bones
you've seen the photos
black and white

trust me, in full colour
it smells like rotting food,
a murder of flies
buzzing the only constant

how we were even able
to put one foot before the other
is its own miracle

after two months of
scrambling for moldy bread
and sucking the mud to ingest
a few drops of spilled soup

there was nothing left of a day
but watching what eyes were
still open

some nights, mother passed me
bits of raw meat she said she found
told me *first close your eyes and pray*

## butcher pack

beef bone-in strip steak
on sale, bright orange best before sticker - tomorrow
four of them, uniform size
well marbled, a thick line of fat along the left edge of each
i must choose one for myself tonight,
freeze the rest for more lean times

*el Milagro de los Andes, 1972*

we need protein in our diets
what few supplies on board the plane are gone,
around us only trees and the lifeless mountains
we begin to contemplate the necessary,
even make jokes,
agreements.
*yes, if i die, you may…*

we swear we saw a prop plane dip its wing
in promise, but after nine days
there were no longer miracles imminent
and through the static of a transistor radio
we learned everyone else had given up.

educated men, once robust and athletic,
we try to reason
debate survival versus taboo
flesh or soul
someone has a bible, finds relevant passages
exemptions

when we are finally ready
four of us take razor blades and glass shards
approach the place we'd buried them face down
i go first, break through the snow and ice,
start with the one on the end.

## *Neteotoquiliztli:* the desire to be regarded as a god

Who can tell my story?
I am gone
and the appropriators have their own language.
Interpretations, agendas.

They call us victims, those destined for the plinth,
our Aztec rituals brutal, condemn us with their histories.

But let me explain our acquiescence:
It was my honour and privilege to lay myself upon the ledge,
inhale the bright sky, blinded by the sun;
I barely saw the knife's glint,
the blessed hands that wrenched my beating heart
from between my breasts and held it up
for the glory of the gods.

Prior to this ceremony there were feasts and festivals
where I was treated as one of them
and now my purpose is to appease, to carry the
needs of my people to the greater powers.
You must believe
I boldly and sincerely gave myself to this calling.

And as my heart dies in the bite of the priest
my body will be tumbled down a hundred temple steps
to be flayed, my skin worn by beggars as royal robes,
my limbs distributed to the worthy.

But my soul is above this,
alive in rapture.
It may be hard to understand
yet do you not tell a similar tale of sacrifice?

## Tim and Vince and the girl in 3C

after a hard hot carnie week,
when you get on a Greyhound in Edmonton,
looking forward to home cooking, mom,
you just want to put the seat back
headphones on, and nod off.
as the other passengers settle in,
smile at one or two, but mind your own business,
barely acknowledge the older guy
who takes the seat beside you in Erikson.
go back to sleep.

you should be in Winnipeg by dinner tomorrow.

midnight bus to Winni, find a friendly,
sleeping face back near the toilet,
then when the voices tell you, take out your knife
to stab the devil in the neck and chest, destroy the evil
never mind the screams as
passengers scramble out onto the cold dark roadside

lock the doors and brandish bleeding head at windows
slash at the glassy faces of would-be heros,
make them watch you savour bits of flesh and eyeballs
make the ladies vomit in the ditch
tell the cops you must stay here forever,
then just throw yourself against the emergency exit, break free
resign yourself to taser, cuffs and

you should be safe in a mental health centre by morning.

it's been six months since you've seen your boyfriend,
can't wait for Winnipeg,
and camping at the lake, catch up on reading, starting now,
row 3, window seat
someone walks by heading to the bathroom, screams.
the driver brakes and shoves you all out to the gravel shoulder
of Yellowhead highway, no bags, jackets, huddle with strangers
then it becomes clear the madman in the bus window
has a heart in his hand

## absolute discharge
*february 10, 2017*

no significant threat, they say
suffering
from undiagnosed schizophrenia at the time,
they say
not criminally responsible.

after nine years
progressing well, they say
treated and released,
is hopeful and cooperative with his doctors
is taking his meds, they say
and attends counseling appointments
wishes to be redeemed.
now he goes by another name, they say.

no doubt some will be fearful, they say
but this is our civilized and compassionate
criminal code.

his victim's mother has nothing to say.

## recovered

a river is convenient--
aside from the obvious
source of all things sustaining
and irrigational,
it is a place
to dispose of the detritus,
the sewage,
the dead.

one must wonder
where they hide the bodies
on the prairie.

# Dahmer

## *(i) intrigue*

what kid hasn't kept insects in jars,
blown up ants on a sunny day
with a magnifying glass
poked at roadkill to
watch the maggots scramble

hid carcasses in the woods
until the dry bones were ready
to rattle in his pockets

what kid hasn't impaled a
dog's head on a stake?

### *(ii) bright and alone*

he was the outcast,
smuggling gin to school
in the lining of his camo jacket,
smart kid, polite, but apathetic.
uninspired talent wasted
on offensive pranks and
merely odd behaviors

make them laugh so
they don't know you like boys,
dream of sabotage and bondage.

### *(iii) his first victim*

this gets messy.

hitchhiker invited in for drinks,
wants to go home
struck from behind and strangled
with a 10 lb dumbbell
his corpse the fetish, used

then dissected:
flesh goes here, in acid
flushed
bones go here, in the back woods
crushed.

## *(iv) jobs*

army medic
deli counter
phlebotomist
chocolate mixer
are we seeing a pattern here?

### *(v) $50 and a leather belt*

for fifty bucks they'll get in your car
turn their back long enough.
you become efficient.
bodies start to pile up.
people notice.

### *(vi) the collector perfecting his craft*

after several accidents with bleach
causing brittle skulls
he reasoned that freezing bones
for several months would remove moisture

this did not work
resulting in a skull shattering in the oven,
bones requiring acid disposal,
disappointment,

back to the original method:
boiling parts
in a large steel kettle of soilex, rinse
the organs and flesh away
for future use

light bleach for 24 hours then
the secret is the week of air drying
on an old bath towel

reassemble skeleton
and paint the severed head, shellac
it's ready for display

### *(vii) cover up*

the neighbours start to complain
you say the freezer broke down, all your meat spoiled.

the next time, you tell the landlord
several of your tropical fish died recently.

promise to buy air freshener.

### *(viii) the one that got away*

this is how to survive:
note the odour and the supply of muriatic acid
on the living room floor, allow the story
about cleaning bricks

appear to cooperate when the handcuffs are slipped on,
but draw the line when a knife is held to your heart
and your captor tells you he wants more than to
take nude photos

your first clue was the posters, then
the exorcist video playing in the background,
and the rot coming from the blue drum in the corner

unbutton your shirt if it will buy time, he's lost in a reverie of
chanting and imagining the taste of your flesh.
as you let him lay his head upon your chest, take account
of all the doors and windows, say you're his friend

ask to use the bathroom,
ask to have a beer in the cool living room
ask to use the bathroom again
punch him in the face and run

***(ix) inventory***

924 North 25th Street Apartment 213 search, July 23, 1991
item: four severed heads found in kitchen
item: seven skulls, bleached, painted, found in bedroom and closet
item: blood drippings in refrigerator drain tray
item: two human hearts and arm muscle in plastic bags on fridge shelves
item: entire torso plus bag of human organs and flesh embedded in freezer ice
item: two entire skeletons
item: one pair severed hands
item: two preserved penises
item: one mummified scalp
item: one 57-gallon drum containing three human torsos in various stages of decomposition in unidentified acid
item: 74 Polaroid pictures of dismembered victims

### *(x) confession*

"I have consumed the hearts,
livers,
thighs
and biceps
of several men
over the past year."

### *(xi) his plan, thwarted*

there was to be a black table
before the dark draped window
an altar of skulls
flanked on each side
by a full skeleton.
there would be incense for mood,
soft blue globe lights
and a comfortable black leather chair
in which he could meditate,
a place where he could feel at home.

### *(xii) retribution*

he shaped prison food into
severed limbs, asked for extra ketchup,
made the guards uneasy.

god told fellow inmate christopher scarver
to take that iron bar beneath his shirt
and fell the monster, leave him
on the bathroom floor to bleed,
there is nothing more to lose.

the guards have all gone on break.
stories change.

### *(xiii) after the candlelight vigils*

it's a vacant lot
his mother dead
his father sued for parental negligence
and there was a brother
who has since changed his name.

that's the thing about names.
nobody remembers the victims.

## the victims

i want to tell you who they were
it's a matter of public record
you can find the list on wikipedia

but
is it something their mothers would want?
i think that gets in the way of acknowledging victims

the shame

is the recognition
celebrity even
for the perpetrator: the marquis de sade, jack the ripper,
boston strangler, ted bundy…

the irony of resting in peace
is that your particular circumstances are
swept under the rug, hushed at family reunions
not brought up for fear
of offending, hurting

yet there are articles and novels and ballads and poems
written about the event,
the reprehensible
thing that happened
people are curious,
scandal and sensationalism is marketable
so evil becomes a household name

## obedience

*here cannibal, cannibal, cannibal*
*here cannibal cannibal*
*here cannibal, cannibal, cannibal*
*here cannibal cannibal*

i thought she was calling her dog.
i thought, what kind of dog?

he came running
across the open field like on tv
he ran
it was a man
it was a man who ran across the open field
leapt on her, threw her down
in the open field

she was down
he was down

i think i was over here
or there

that's almost exactly what took place
in this or that very place

where she called him, said
*come*
*cannibal,*
*cannibal, come*

yes, she asked him.
she told him
she wanted

*here, cannibal,*
*there there,*

he stopped at bone.

## dog eat dog

"may contain animal byproducts"
at least those are the ingredients i can pronounce.

my coonhounds don't care
nor have i shown them the videos
of chicken feet and bull testicles
being scraped off the floor and tossed in the grinder,
dried and chopped into fake gravy laced little cubes
to be sold in a bright red bag
on the bottom shelf at walmart.

there's a spot they've discovered in the field
where someone puts out bait
for rabbits, foxes, coyotes,
whatever comes along.
they will eat anything
if they get there before i can stop them.
they leave the carrots and lettuce but
sometimes find a femur or jawbone to flaunt.

like to pretend they're wolves,
bay wildly as they defend their kill.

## decapitation

such a skinny little neck
his (presumably) claws/talons/fists
thrashing at me like a pugilist
*outclassed*, i tell him.

if vertical he would be a stickman but
in my firm two-fingered clinch his armpits pulsate
with what i think may be a heartbeat,
i briefly consider dissection,
after
just to understand the mechanics

and so test his eyes, note a tiny black iris
wandering independently of the other--
such clever surveillance tactics
or inattention.
i expect my close-up face is also triangular
as he reaches forward with legs one and two,
around behind with leg three
(to snare my middle finger,)
kicks numbly with leg four,
while five and six pedal, flex, attempt
anything.

then long wings begin to splay largeness
inflict terror and intimidation,
that brown under-cloak unfolding means
business
*ho hum* i soon tire and put him back
on solid ground, crawl down to his level,
look him in the compound eyes
and feign a one-two in order to assess his
reaction time
the little coward turns and skitters off,
- quite a coordinated retreat

unfinished, i pounce, and once more
take his thorax in my pinch to
safely set him out of lawnmower range
his brilliant camouflage ill-placed on silver birch,
his meandering still observable.

## carpe eat ‘um

there’s one goldfish missing.
goober. a pretty calico fantail,
disappeared four days ago.

likely stranded in the rocks
or under the pond plants. i’ve looked.
ruled out raccoons and herons.

i anticipate pieces will begin to surface
in a week or so.
his buddies will clean up after him.

## the placenta eater

oh, who died? right, the
placenta eater. hippie.
long hair, flowered skirts…
her legacy an anecdote:

yes, she kept it in the freezer.
sliced off bits for stew,
offered it to guests.

what does one say?
there are children at the table,
must set an example, be gracious.

fill up on bread,
ask for more wine,

note the smell of that
apple pie on the counter.
insist you must save room
for dessert.

wish i'd gotten to know her better.
she was a lovely girl.

## why mothers should be allowed to eat their young

*Arrested development differs from arrested growth,*
*as parts in the former state continue to grow whilst*
*still retaining their early condition.*
*Various monstrosities come under this head,*
*and some are known to be occasionally inherited...*
*- C. Darwin, Descent of Man*

once the chicken is in the egg,
the decision is already made
as to what it's going to be
DNA to zygote to fetus,
to adult

so if we knew our offspring
would be deformed
or would be born
corrupt and murderous
would we as mother
choose to do the honorable thing
for the survival of the species?

nurture arguments say
society created the rapist
and the child killer, but
how does his momma feel
witnessing his deathwatch
on the late news, waiting for
the activists to win
a stay of execution,

does she wish now she'd eaten off
the vernix-covered head
like a rodent?

**mana**

rumour has it
Polynesians in Marquesas
eat high ranking enemies
to absorb their power

they call this mana
but it's protein, nonetheless

recipe:
break legs to prevent eat and run
break arms to discourage thrashing about
break ribs inward to puncture lungs, a quiet meal
impale on a rough tree trunk ass to mouth and

well, now you have a spitting image;
stoke the fire!

particular body parts are favoured
savoured
pissing off the victims' families
who seek retribution
eye for an eye sort of thing
- guess who's coming to dinner next week?

never ending circle of life, notes the anthropologist,
and the population is dwindling.

## taboo

*Capt. James Cook, d. Feb. 14, 1779*

an injustice has been done
to the people of hawaii
a gross assault
on their reputation
perpetrated by western colonial ideologies
to appease christian sensibilities
and the missionary position:
*these beautiful islands must be saved!*

it was a mere miscommunication
a cultural misunderstanding
a small tiff
that got out of hand:

captain cook clubbed to death by
restless natives,
the crew appalled
to find his charred filets
shared among the local aristocracy.

yet their intentions were purely honorable,
how dreadful to accuse them of such savagery
against a man of obvious distinction.

no, indeed his meat's a token of supremacy,
a favour bestowed
upon an illustrious chief

how dare you think we'd eat him!

sirs, do join us at the feast and be assured
it's just his goose we cooked.

## long pig

our podgy dinner companion wears sunglasses
& a straw hat,
is dressed appropriately for a luau, bright
florals, fruit garnish, fresh off the catamaran cliché;
he's such a cut-up, this should be so much fun!

i hardly recognized the guest of honour
from earlier that morning
when he'd been carried in like royalty on a bamboo spit
by two hot shirtless natives, employees of the resort
entrusted with such pomp & ceremony.

now he lounges on a bier
strewn with banana leaves, ringed by pineapple &
poi pots, orchids & papaya, grass skirted dancing girls
while mai tai happy tourists take selfies next to him.

oh, what a time they are having, those women
sporting plumeria behind correct ears,
men making jokes about getting leid
while postcard sunset drums & ukulele ambience
surround the beach like tiki torches.

and don ho's stand-in talks about the culture,
explains the roasting process step by step as
gaping mouths begin to salivate when sweet decadent
smoke now signals serving time
is imminent

but where is mr. chester white? i see his hat
and sunglasses…

## on viewing video of pig in black bikini

don’t eat pig
don’t pig out
don’t be a pig
don’t eat with your mouth open
don’t eat pig with open mouth
don’t open your mouth
don’t talk about pig
don’t out pig
out, pig! out!

## *suidae domesticus:* the pig

the grunting, suckling pig,
guzzled and groaned
'til the poor baby could take no more.
but still, he desired,
for the essence of a pig is greed.
yet the wild boar
bites my hand
as i reach out to fulfill
all his desires.

*suidae domesticus*
raised and stuffed, aye, for a purpose.
'though he fights his own fate, his very pigness
leads him to the slaughter,
and oh, the muscles of his pleasure
would delight any man.

**fudge**

he brought me candy,
maple, buttercream and
chocolate fudge samples in a
white paper bag,  and the first
piece i consumed voraciously,

the second, guiltily

but then he began to insist
i have more, and he began to tell
me  i liked it, i must like it, all
women love chocolate

teasing,
he tried to force it past my lips
so i bit his finger

## the obscenity of consummation

it starts with the eyes,
ah, there's a tasty dish,
he thought
as he devoured her
just with his eyes…

starving for affection
he thought,
delectable

nibbles and love bites
she thought
delicious

satisfaction
she thought,
yes, say yes

knead, sniff, taste, suck
flesh on flesh

teeth, bones
nip, gnaw, swallow
sweet nectar
guzzle and gorge

insatiable gluttons,
they thought

## carrion

bleeding still
fresh like last night
reliving death dismembered
and impersonal
the way you always did
devour me.

i see you hover in
what is left of sight
a perverse eclipse over
my face, my face reflected

and now you peck,
eyelid and through and breast
as i lay rotting
in your path.

if my wings were not severed,
splayed and useless
i could fly
but you found me this way;
it was so easy, no killing
was necessary

and now that the best is gone,
you still gorge on my
remnants. naked, sun-broiled.

## cold

piece of my heart?
pound of flesh?
whatever.
bite me, baby,
i can take it.

gave my right arm
shirt off back
hand up.

got lip service
got black eyes
got burned before.

try me.
bring it.
i can take you.

## a dinner conversation

you say this
exotica
tastes like chicken,
but what did chicken taste like
before everything tasted
like chicken?

we saw possum roadkill
on our way to dinner
--hey, if you were in Arkansas,
...it would taste
like
chicken, i guess

i asked you intimately, over dessert
“honey, what do i taste like?”

and you didn’t answer,
chicken!

## vivisection

*A group of six or seven of these hideous reptiles may often be seen*
*on the black rocks a few feet above the surf, basking in the sun*
*with outstretched legs. I opened the stomachs of several…*
*Charles Darwin. Albamare Island, Galapagos, September 29, 1835*

i)

i'm on a beach, in a strange place and the inhabitants seem
welcoming,
how better to get to know these aliens, than to dine—
hot, spicy, it's all subjective,
but at least i'm willing to sample the world's epicure;
i know so many people who will only order spaghetti, or chicken,
no matter what restaurant they're in – i often assume illiteracy,
if not cainotophobia – they expect some form of chicken or pasta
on every menu—
this is safe, comfort food, to bridge that awkward language gap

i have a friend who noted that in every village he visited,
in every language
he has discovered a variation of flour cooked in oil,
(some with fillings)
this is how we learn about other cultures—
slice right in
get to the meat
break bread

ii)

i'm on a local beach
populated by hideous reptiles.
they are shameless male specimens trudging and dripping
glistening bloated exo-spandex bellies displayed,
practically invite deeper scrutiny;
they seem so unadapted to this environment.

iii)

i opened the stomach and found: moss, lichen
birds indigenous to four islands over,
an illinois plate, 2 (mismatched) sneakers,
another stomach, the dog's breakfast,
the dog,
a pearl,
jonah

## don't bite my head off

it's funny
how funny
it is
not nervous laughter but
snickers and guffaws
the jokes on you
smoke's on you
stoke the fire!

raise the ire of tight assed
liberals concerned with implications
racist propaganda
anthropologists correcting
cultural appropriation
inappropriate assumptions

even though it happens
everywhere, from mantis to
black widow
dog eat dog and
people-eating people

just admit it,
light meat, dark meat,

chewing fat is oral mastication
and gnawing an armbone
humerus.

## family dinner

finger foods and canapés
stuffed and devilled
roe, paté
washed down with bloody marys.

light meat or dark?
back or thigh?
gizzards tripe
a sweet brown eye?
sausage headcheese
who wants the pope's fat nose?

side dishes
baked scalloped boiled
chilled pickled presented
in crystal bowls or casseroles
with names taped to the bottoms.

desserts
fruity creamy succulent
fattening frivolous opulent
mince pies and cherry trifles, tarts

…we rest in peace with digestifs
until the guest of honour farts.

## Word of mouth

Said the cannibal, tongue in cheek:
I'm sorry I put my foot in mouth,
but bite your lip!
You don't have to jump down my throat.

Really, what's the saying?
An eye for an eye?
He treated me like a piece of meat.
Lucky I didn't give him a knuckle sandwich.
I have a gut feeling you
gotta have a thick skin in this business --
keep your eyes peeled, try not to get cold feet,
or butterfingers.

Don't mean to talk your ear off
but I'm boiling mad and I needed to
pick someone's brains.
Young blood like you, you don't understand.
what it's like to barely get by
by the skin of your teeth, keep your head above water.

There were times I'd give an arm and a leg --
bun in the oven, brain drain, no stomach for
yesterday's breakfast –
yet if I had to stab someone in the back to save face
vs. bottom out,
well, eat your heart out, it's no freckles off my nose.

Now, now! Don't be getting' a chip on your shoulder,
(And over my dead body NEVER
put anything bigger than an elbow in your ear!)
I'm only pulling your leg.
(But that asshole's ears must be burning!)

## apocalypse

blame george romero
this cult of flesh eating
voyeurism pseudo mystic
consumption

raw lust  rot fresh
meat special effects and saturday
midnight screenings

wobble down main streets crazy
ragged  brainless
glee
near glee
the mad party of
acceptance
normalization
arms reaching out clichés

this used to be in books of law and mores
thou shalt nots
yes
it was that common,
no never
no never
we do not speak
of things that happened of necessity or
insanity

we did not

neanderthals and famished isolates
the flotsam of the shipping age
thin and pious missionaries intent on bringing
civility to new guinea

the crazy guy on the subway,
or the old woman in the woods who made
little tarts of fashion models just three years ago.
shocking. shocking, no?
but you keep reading,

tune in at 11.  a man chewed off
his mother's face. in texas.

now is the experimental edge of
how far
how much horror terror taboo
can a society stretch

call good fun

push back push back
the line keeps pushing back
wait there's more

it hasn't yet gone live

## just desserts (on the anticipation of feedback)

…and now come the critics:

the epicurious
the perverse and decadent,
true gastronomists,

or the connoisseurs of fine literature
who would cannibalize my work

so to them
i simply say,
"fork it!"

# Acknowledgements

*suidae domesticus*: the pig appeared in *secrets of the unicorn* (St. Clair College Press, 1974)

The naturalist appeared in *Room of One's Own – Geek Girls*, September 2014

dream – Mimi the Potbelly Pig appeared in *smack in the middle of spotlit obvious* (Urban Farmhouse Press, 2016)

Thanks to my publisher Daniel Lockhart for saying, "Hey, cool, write more!"; Karen R and Karen T for stomaching the raw poems; Sara for nonchalantly telling the guy at Chapters she needed a copy of "Cannibalism" by Bill Schutt for me for Mother's Day; and John B. Lee for feeding me constant encouragement

# About the Author

Laurie Smith holds a B.Ed and M.A. in Creative Writing from the University of Windsor. An editor and writing coach, she facilitates workshops and is co-publisher of Cranberry Tree Press. Over the years she's won several poetry prizes, including 3rd place in the Great Canadian Panty Poem contest and first place in the Leonard Cohen Old Ideas contest, plus first place in short stories for the Detroit Tri-centennial Writing Competition and the Literary Arts Windsor Chapbook Competition. Collections include *The Truth about Roller Skating* (CTP, 2011) and *smack in the middle of spotlit obvious* (Urban Farmhouse Press, 2016). She's currently working on several projects and acknowledges the support of the Ontario Arts Council. Smith does like her steak rare.

CPSIA information can be obtained
at www.ICGtesting.com
Printed in the USA
LVOW11s0848201017
553134LV00001B/3/P